Multicultural Children's Literature

Authors, Illustrators, & Activities

By
Shirley Norby
and
Gregory Ryan

Cover and Inside Illustrations by
Darcy Myers

Publishers
T.S. Denison & Company, Inc.
Minneapolis, Minnesota 55431

DEDICATIONS

For the Dream Makers of all races
who create and guide others to all that is beautiful;
and for my brother, David, teacher and guide to young people.
Where there is love, there is lasting beauty.

S.N.

For Liz, Caitlin, and Abigail.
For friends, near and far.
For Albert Einstein who said,
"L'imagination est plus importante que la connaissance."

G.R.

T.S. DENISON & COMPANY, INC.

Standard Book Number: 513-02234-1
Multicultural Children's Literature
Copyright © 1994 by T.S. Denison & Co., Inc.
9601 Newton Avenue South
Minneapolis, Minnesota 55431

INTRODUCTION

This is the fifth in our series of books about the women and men who have created many of the best-loved children's books of all time. It combines biographical information, photographs, and suggested book related activities.

No doubt, you will recognize the names of many of these authors and illustrators as having won such prestigious awards as the Newbery and Caldecott Medals. As you read, you will learn where and when they were born, where they grew up and went to school, and how and why they came to create the books which have touched the hearts of so many children around the world.

We believe that an exposure to high-quality books can serve to develop in children not only an appreciation for peoples and customs from other cultures, but also a keener appreciation for the diversity found in our own culture.

We have worked together as a teacher and librarian in a small coastal New Jersey elementary school for almost twenty-five years. One of our greatest pleasures has been to bring children and books together. For a long time we had looked for a book about authors and illustrators to share with our inquisitive students, but we could not find one that was just right for their age group. So we decided to write such a book: *Famous Children's Authors*. That was soon followed by *Famous Children's Authors, Book II*, *Famous Children's Authors Activities*, and *Famous Illustrators of Children's Literature*. We hope that the book you hold in your hands will serve as a springboard for developing your own interest in children's literature. We also hope it will help you to share your interest with as many children as possible.

Shirley Norby
Gregory Ryan

Table of Contents

MITSUMASA ANNO

There were no picture books for children when Mitsumasa Anno was growing up and going to school in the small town of Tsuwano in western Japan. Anno loved to draw, though, so his imagination was always very active. "I just love drawing," he says, "That's all."

Anno was a good student. He was also a good artist. So good, in fact, that once he was scolded in school because he made play money that looked too real!

When he graduated from the Yamagushi Teacher Training College he became an art teacher in the early grades. While in his twenties, Anno became an editor for a children's encyclopedia. Some years later, he decided to leave teaching to give himself entirely to creating children's books.

Since Anno had always been interested in very young children and how they learn, it is not surprising that his first books were designed for children who could not yet read. These books show that Anno's imagination is full of twisting paths that take his "readers" on unusual travels.

Anno's Journey is a book filled with drawings that look just like a walk through the woods. When you look more closely, though, you see that the paths and trees are filled with over a hundred unusual and delicate birds, animals, and people. It's like parting a curtain of leaves in the forest to see what's hidden there. Only this curtain is also the curtain of your imagination. The more carefully you look at Anno's pictures, the more you find. He knows that the more you use your imagination, the more you will want to use it.

Anno's Aesop is a story of a story. Little Freddy Fox finds a book of Aesop's Fables, but since he can't read he doesn't realize what he has found. Freddy shows it to his father, Mr. Fox, who uses only the pictures in the book (not the words) *and* his imagination to tell the stories of the Fables. When he does this he winds up with brand new stories! Aesop told the stories one way 2500 years ago. Mr. Fox told them another way. Not a *wrong* way—just another way. This is just fine with Anno. He believes that people should trust their minds and hearts while they learn about the world. They are very good guides and will often lead you more surely than what some books might tell you.

Anno's artwork has earned him awards all over the world. Even so, he told us that his proudest moments were when his son and daughter were born. Anno lives with his family near Tokyo.

Anno told us that if he could have three wishes he would wish this way: "Please grant me three more wishes. And make it thrice. And once more make it thrice!"

Our wish would be for Anno to: "Please make three more books. And make it thrice. And once more make it thrice!"

A Selection of Books Written and Illustrated by Mitsumasa Anno

Anno's Aesop
Anno's Alphabet
Anno's Animals
Anno's Britain
Anno's Counting Book
Anno's Counting House
Anno's Flea Market
Anno's Hat Tricks
Anno's Italy
Anno's Journey
Anno's Magical Alphabet
Anno's Math Games
Anno's Medieval World
Anno's Mysterious Multiplying Jar
Anno's U.S.A.
Dr. Anno's Magical Midnight Circus
Topsy-Turvies: Pictures to Stretch the Imagination
The King's Flower
Upside-Downers: More Pictures to Stretch the Imagination

Activities
Mitsumasa Anno

1. Choose any one of your favorite picture books. Look at the pictures in a new way and think of a whole new story to go with the pictures. Tell your story to a friend.

2. Read *Anno's Counting Book*. Take five pieces of drawing paper and fold them in half to make a little book. Hold them together with a staple or a piece of yarn. Draw a cover for your own counting book. Call it: *(Your Name)'s Counting Book*. Inside, draw pictures that would show 0,1,2,3,4... Share your book with a younger friend and talk about the pictures.

3. Read Anno's book *The King's Flower*. Notice how BIG some things look. The King's servants need pulleys to help pick up his knife and fork so he can eat. Draw a picture where ordinary things look GIGANTIC. How would a person use them? Tell a story about your picture and how everything got that way.

4. *Anno's U.S.A.* takes the reader backwards in time during a journey through the United States. Choose a modern invention such as the television set and draw pictures of what televisions used to look like through the years. Imagine what they might look like in the future. Do this for other inventions: radio, telegraph, spaceships, cars, computers. Think of others yourself.

JOSE ARUEGO

Jose Aruego was born in Manila, the capital of the Philippines on August 9, 1932. As a youngster, Jose loved to draw and was especially interested in comic book art. He collected comic books and even rented them to his friends. In school he was known for his ability to decorate the walls of classrooms with his line drawings.

The young Jose loved to "doodle" by making squiggly line drawings of animals. He spent his summers on a farm outside Manila where there were many animals and he had several pets. Readers often notice how playful his animals appear in the books he illustrates. He combines his love of humor and animals with bright, bold colors to create characters that express human feelings.

Jose's father and sister were lawyers and his family wanted him to study law also. He agreed and became a lawyer but what he really wanted to be was a comic book and cartoon artist. He practiced law for only three months and then went to New York to study graphic arts and advertising art. His family understood his wish to make art his career and helped him to make the change.

In New York City Jose attended the Parsons School of Design. He worked for several design studios and magazines and did a great deal of traveling. When he first arrived in New York he was lonesome for his family and friends but he gradually adjusted and in 1961 married another artist, Ariane Dewey. They had one son, Juan, whose name appears in their book, *Juan and the Asuangs*. Jose has dedicated all his books to his son who is an adult now. Juan lives in Germany where he writes for magazines and newspapers.

Jose and Ariane Dewey Aruego collaborated on writing and illustrating many children's books. They were divorced in 1973 but continue to work together although now Ariane uses her maiden name, Ariane Dewey.

Jose Aruego lives and works in an apartment in New York City where he has a studio. Like *Milton the Early Riser*, he gets up very early in the morning. He draws and paints in the morning and spends his afternoons doing research. He usually is working on several book projects at the same time.

He says that he feels very much like an American now although he still visits the Philippines. Tropical plants, animals, and Philippine folklore and culture frequently appear in his stories and drawings.

In 1976 Jose Aruego was honored by his former country as "Outstanding Filipino Abroad in the Arts." Many of his law professors and classmates were at the ceremony to congratulate him on his success as a children's book illustrator. Changing careers for Jose Aruego and for his fans throughout the world has turned out to be a wise decision. Like *Leo the Late Bloomer*, he has found success and happiness while doing work he loves.

A Selection of Books Illustrated or Written by
Jose Aruego

Another Mouse to Feed
Boris Bad Enough
Chick and the Duckling
Come Out and Play, Little Mouse
Crocodile's Tale: A Philippine Folk Story
Dance Away
Gregory, the Terrible Eater
Juan and the Asuangs: A Tale of Philippine Ghosts & Spirits
King and His Friends
Leo the Late Bloomer
The Lizard's Story
Look What I Can Do
Marie Louise and Christophe
Marie Louise and Christophe at the Carnival
Marie Louise's Heyday
Mert the Blurt
Milton, the Early Riser
Mitchell Is Moving
Mouse Work
Musical Max
Noel the Coward
One Duck, Another Duck
Owliver
Rockabye Crocodile
Sea Frog, City Frog
Surprise?
Symbiosis: A Book of Unusual Friendships
Three Friends
Two Greedy Bears
We Hide, You Seek
Where Are You Going Little Mouse?
Where Does the Sun Go at Night?
Whose Mouse Are You?

Activities
Jose Aruego

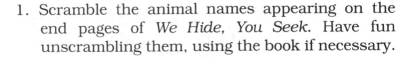

1. Scramble the animal names appearing on the end pages of *We Hide, You Seek*. Have fun unscrambling them, using the book if necessary.

2. Read *Herman the Helper*. With colored markers recreate an imaginative underwater scene encouraging young artists to use non-traditional colors for the fish and marine life.

3. Pandas like *Milton the Early Riser* need special diets of bamboo to live. As bamboo disappears, the natural habitats for pandas are lost. Research why bamboo forests are disappearing and the problems zoos face raising pandas in captivity.

4. A Bulletin Board Idea: Draw an outline of a large ark and fill it with Aruego's animals. Use magic markers to recreate the bright colors of his illustrations.

5. Use *Rockabye Crocodile* to make children aware that the American crocodile is on the endangered species list. Investigate why and when they became endangered and what products are made from crocodile skins. List substitutes that could be used to produce the same articles without killing any crocodiles.

6. Anxious parents of a "late bloomer" wonder why their son can't do anything right in *Leo the Late Bloomer*, a gentle, comforting story written by Robert Kraus and illustrated by Jose Aruego. Share the book with parents and children who need a boost in self esteem and confidence. Discuss how being different can be uncomfortable; whether those differences are developmental, cultural, racial, etc.

LEO and DIANE DILLON

Illustrators Leo and Diane Dillon were both born in March, 1933 but in states far apart. Diane grew up in Glendale, California; Leo in Brooklyn, New York. They met after high school when the were attending the Parsons School of Design in New York City. They fell in love and were married in 1957.

As children they loved to draw. A family friend encouraged Leo's interest in art by taking him to visit artist's homes and sharing their books and drawings with him. Leo's mother bought him his first paint set when he was nine. Diane's parents encouraged her talent and usually gave her art supplies for Christmas. She recalls receiving her first oil paint set in a wooden carrying case when she was eleven and thereafter feeling like a "real" artist. Leo and Diane have always known that they wanted to be artists.

Today the Dillons work in studios inside their Brooklyn, New York home. They work almost every day, even on holidays and weekends. Their grown-up son, Lee, also has a studio in the house where he sculpts, paints, and makes jewelry. Sometimes he assists his parents with a design or painting.

Leo and Diane Dillon do a lot of thinking, talking, and research before they become excited enough to begin work on a project. Often they experiment for weeks with new techniques before they feel that their work is "right" for a particular manuscript. Although they work in separate studios, they collaborate on every piece by passing it back and forth, incorporating their sketches into one final illustration. They like to listen to music while they work.

The Dillons have two cats, a Siamese named Dally and a tiger cat called Spats who is pictured perched on a witch's shoulder in a book they illustrated called, *The Porcelain Cat*. Occasionally they use their son, Lee, family friends or even themselves as models.

Readers with keen eyes will notice that sometimes the artists will include the same small detail on several pages of a particular book. Observe the red bird in *Why Mosquitoes Buzz in People's Ears*, and the lions in *Who's in Rabbit's House?* They do this to add humor and reader interest to the pictures.

Why Mosquitoes Buzz in People's Ears, won the Caldecott Medal in 1976. They won again in 1977 for *Ashanti to Zulu: African Traditions*. The Dillons consider winning the Caldecott Medals two of their proudest moments. Despite all the awards and recognition they have earned for their beautiful books, they both say that they want to "get better at what we do."

A Selection of Books Illustrated by
Leo and Diane Dillon

Aida
Ashanti to Zulu: African Traditions
Brother to the Wind
The Color Wizard
Happy Birthday Grampie
Honey, I Love: and Other Love Poems
The Hundred Penny Box
Many Thousand Gone: African Americans from Slavery to Freedom
Moses & Noah's Ark: Stories from the Bible
The People Could Fly: American Black Folktales
Pish, Posh, Said Hieronymus Bosch
The Porcelain Cat
Song of the Boat
The Sorcerer's Apprentice
The Tale of the Mandarin Ducks
Who's in Rabbit's House?: A Masai Tale
Why Mosquitoes Buzz in People's Ears: A West African Tale

Activities
Leo and Diane Dillon

1. Read *Who's in Rabbit's House?* (Verna Aardema/the Dillons). Draw the frame of a house with various rooms on a large piece of poster board. Older children might want to include houses from other parts of the world. Let students go through old magazines and catalogs and cut out the furniture, toys, food, animals, people, etc. that traditionally belong in their houses. Wall decorations can be made with crayons, markers, or from wallpaper sample books. Decorate the outside area or yard in a manner suited to the locale of the homes. This activity adapts easily into small group work and may be expanded and integrated into a social studies "houses and children around the world" project.

2. Incorporate the story of *Aida* into your study of ancient Egypt. Play a recording of the famous "Triumphal March" from the opera for students. Scenes from *Aida* and ancient Egypt make stunning carved plaster bas-relief plaques. Ask the art teacher for assistance with this project. It takes time and space but is well worth the effort.

3. Develop a critical reading and thinking project for older readers by having them compare and contrast *The Tale of the Mandarin Ducks* (Paterson/Dillons) with Hans Christian Andersen's *The Nightingale*. Divide the class into groups to brainstorm after stories are read. Set a time limit and ask each group to appoint a recorder. Orally share the results of small group discussions with the entire class. Sharing a bag of fortune cookies is an enjoyable way to end this activity.

4. *Why Mosquitoes Buzz in People's Ears* and *Who's in Rabbits House?* (both by Verna Aardema and the Dillons) are easily adapted to classroom dramatizations in cooperative activities incorporating art and music. Each story provides many roles for students to play. Costume and scenery requirements are minimal. Simple eye masks tied to children's heads make adequate costumes for the animal, bird and insect characters in both books. Laminate the masks or seal them between sheets of clear Con-Tact paper to preserve and strengthen them. Non-speaking performers may participate by being part of the scenery (trees) or by providing sound effects to heighten the drama of each story.

5. *Many Thousand Gone: African Americans from Slavery to Freedom*, written by Virginia Hamilton and beautifully illustrated by the Dillons recounts the stories of people who attempted to free themselves from slavery. Obtain a copy of a companion book, *Get on Board: The Story of the Underground Railroad* by Jim Haskins (Scholastic). Readers will meet some of the same people who are featured in the Hamilton book but will also find other details and many photographs. Both books are very useful source material for middle and upper grades.

TOM FEELINGS

Tom Feelings' most frequent subjects are African American people. He has said that he wants his art to tell African American children about their roots, "that America is not the world, that elsewhere African American children are living in whole families and with a communal relationship."

Tom Feelings was born in Brooklyn, New York and has been drawing since he was four or five years old. He started by copying characters from comic books and newspapers and inventing stories to go along with his pictures. When he was about nine he met an African American artist who was teaching near Tom's home. This professional artist encouraged him to draw and paint the people and places that were part of Tom's community. He took that advice seriously and wherever he travels and lives, he draws the people of that community as they really are.

Following graduation from high school, he attended the School of Visual Arts and served four years in the U.S. Air Force. He created a comic strip series and worked as a freelance artist from 1958–1964. His subjects were the people of his community which he drew anywhere he found them. In later years he went to the American South and Africa where, through his drawings, he portrayed the people that he found there. He has said that the two years he spent in Ghana resulted in some of the most meaningful and rewarding experiences of his life. He met his former wife, Muriel, in Africa where she was teaching. Together they collaborated on two *Swahili* books, *Jambo Means Hello, An Alphabet Book* and *Moja Means One, A Counting Book.* Both books have won many prestigious awards including being named Caldecott Honor books.

Today, Tom Feelings lives alone in South Carolina in a small house where he has a studio. His two grown sons live with their mother near Philadelphia. He works in his studio all day unless he is teaching. Besides drawing and painting he also does some sculpture. He says that he gets his ideas from looking at and observing everything he can see and hear and from books, television, and movies. His advice to illustrators is, "Carry a sketchbook wherever you go because it's a record of what you're seeing and feeling."

A Selection of Books Illustrated by:
Tom Feelings

African Crafts
African American Pilgrimage
Daydreamers
Folktales
Jambo Means Hello, A Swahili Alphabet Book
Moja Means One: A Swahili Counting Book
Now Sheba Sings the Song
Something on My Mind
Soul Looks Back in Wonder
To Be A Slave

Activities
Tom Feelings

1. Make your own counting and alphabet books. Use *Moja Means One,* and *Jambo Means Hello,* to lead students into their own ethnic and racial heritage research. Create counting and alphabet books that reflect their roots. Illustrations could reflect past or present day life of their heritage.

2. Creative letter writing. Tom Feelings illustrated *To Be a Slave,* written by Julius Lester who also appears in this book. Read the biographical information about both men and imagine the correspondence that might have taken place between them before the publication of *To Be a Slave.* Divide the class into authors and illustrators to get different perspectives and points of view.

3. Community Awareness. Tom Feelings draws what he sees and knows based on his sense of community. Wherever he lives his illustrations reflect everyday actions and life of the people he sees. Ask students to look carefully at their community. What would Tom Feelings see there? What do you think he would choose to illustrate? Would you be proud to see illustrations of life in your community? What wouldn't you be proud to see? If you were the illustrator what would you change about your community? Draw or design a postcard illustration that accurately portrays life in your community.

4. Tom Feelings has collected and illustrated poetry of the African American experience in his book, *Soul Looks Back in Wonder.* He used colored pencils, colored paper, stencil cut-outs and other techniques to give a collage effect for the illustrations. Find poetry that captures the experience of any group of people and illustrate the examples with original drawings, painting, or collage.

GYO FUJIKAWA

Gyo Fujikawa was born in Berkeley, California in 1908. She was the daughter of Hikozo and Yu Fujikawa. Her father, who was a translator for a large seafood company, named her after a famous Chinese emperor. Her mother was a writer. Since Gyo and her brother lived with their parents in an Asian kind of home but went to regular American schools, they grew up with a strong love for both America and Japan.

Gyo always had a talent for art. After high school, she attended an Art Institute in Los Angeles. While she was completing her own studies, she taught classes in painting and design. She thought it was important that people never stop learning, even when they do not go to school anymore.

In the 1930's Gyo worked in the advertising department at the Disney Studios. Her biggest assignment was putting together a book about the movie *Fantasia*. After that, she worked on many other Disney books. She did not stay there very long, though. She went to work for an advertising company in New York.

When World War II broke out some people in the United States were fearful of Japanese-Americans. Gyo was well-liked, though, and she was able to keep her job. She was even offered a better job at another advertising company.

While Gyo was working with the advertising company, a children's book editor asked her to illustrate, *A Child's Garden of Verses,* by Robert Louis Stevenson. She worked at both jobs at the same time because she was not sure that small children would like her artwork. It turned out that they liked her work so much that she was hired to illustrate many other books.

Gyo became famous for her pictures of babies. Their faces were so adorable that people simply fell in love with them. Her paintings appeared in books, magazines, and on baby food labels.

Gyo was invited to use her talent to design several stamps for the United States Postal Service. One of her paintings was used on a stamp to celebrate the fiftieth anniversary of the International Peace Garden. This is not surprising because when you look at Gyo's paintings you get the feeling that all the characters really care for each other. Even the trolls, elves, gnomes, goblins, and fairies!

Gyo's artwork has kept her so busy that on some days she never even leaves her studio. Over the past forty years she has created over thirty books which are enjoyed by children in America, Japan, and eighteen other countries.

A Selection of Books Illustrated by
Gyo Fujikawa

A Child's Book of Poems
A Child's Garden of Verses
A to Z Picture Book
Are You My Friend Today?
Babies
Baby Animals
Can You Count?
Come Follow Me...To the Secret World of Elves and Fairies and Gnomes and Trolls
Fairy Tales and Fables
Jenny Learns a Lesson
Let's Eat
Let's Play
Millie's Secret
Mother Goose
My Favorite Thing
The Night Before Christmas
Oh, What a Busy Day!
Sleepy Times
That's Not Fair!
Welcome Is a Wonderful Word

Activities
Gyo Fujikawa

1. Design an ABC picture book. Fold sheets of drawing paper in half to make the pages. Design a cover for "*(Your Name)'s A to Z Picture Book.*" Draw one or two large letters on each page and add drawings of people, places, or things that begin with that letter.

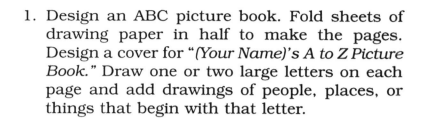

2. Assemble a collection of colorful postage stamps. Design a stamp for your school or class. Choose symbols which will represent things that are important to you. Draw the stamp large-size, then shrink it down to stamp-size using a photocopy machine. Use the stamps on class notes and letters.

3. Invent a name for a new line of baby food products and create a poster to advertise it. Tell why your food is better than food sold by other companies. Be sure to include the adorable face of a very satisfied customer.

4. Select several of your favorite poems. Copy them onto paper which you have folded into a book. Draw pictures to go with the poems. Make cardboard covers for your book and share it with a friend.

5. Read *Baby Animals*. A baby swan is called a cygnet. A baby horse is called a foal. Find the names of the other animals. Write the names of the grown-up animals in one column; write the names of the babies in another column. Mix them up for a friend to match in the right way.

VIRGINIA HAMILTON

Virginia Hamilton, famous storyteller and novelist, was born and raised in Yellow Springs, Ohio, which was once a station on the Underground Railroad. Her grandfather had been a fugitive slave who settled in Yellow Springs after escaping from slavery. Virginia's parents owned a small farm but didn't have much money. They raised all their own food with enough left over to sell to a grocery store. Virginia was the youngest of five children and she had many uncles, aunts, and cousins who lived nearby. When they weren't busy in the fields they liked to gather to tell stories, gossip, and sing about their ancestors, neighbors, and one another.

Virginia loved to listen to them and grew up with a great deal of pride and knowledge of her own family history. Her childhood in Yellow Springs was happy and she has lived there all her life except for a period of fifteen years when she lived in New York City. She lives there now with her husband, Arnold Adoff, who is a poet and their two children, Leigh and Jaime.

Virginia Hamilton is best known for her young adult books although she has also written biographies, books for younger readers and has retold African American folktales and creation stories from around the world for readers of all ages. She was the first African American woman to win the Newbery Award for *M.C. Higgins, the Great.* Two other titles, *The Planet of Junior Brown,* and *Sweet Whispers, Brother Rush,* were named Newbery Honor books. She has won many other awards as well.

Virginia Hamilton has said that she doesn't sit down at her typewriter determined to write an African American story, but since she is African American and she knows African American people she is comfortable writing about the people she knows best. More important than race and color are the issues her book's characters address. Her stories are about friendship, family relationships, traditions, individual freedom, emotions, and feelings all people experience. Many of her book characters are survivors who undergo some type of journey or quest before they gain freedom and understanding. Her books are often realistic, sometimes mysterious, and never boring!

In, *The People Could Fly*, she has retold African American folktales in a way that is meaningful to many people. The stories relate how slaves disguised themselves and took on names of animals as a means of protection when they gathered together. When they escaped, the idea of "people who could fly" was born. Flight and freedom were synonymous.

Virginia Hamilton likes to drive her car and will often use her car to travel instead of airplanes. She finds it relaxing to look at fellow travelers on the road, especially those with children. Sometimes her automobile trips give her ideas for a new story. She says that she can write anywhere but finds writing hard work. When she gets tired or frustrated over a writing project she takes a break by going out in her car for a drive.

This famous author writes that we should all remember the voices and stories of our past because they are a part of our heritage and history. Her books help us to understand history and ourselves.

A Selection of Books by Virginia Hamilton

The All Jahdu Storybook
Anthony Burns: The Defeat & Triumph of a Fugitive Slave
Arilla Sun Down
Bells of Christmas
Cousins
The Dark Way: Stories of the Spirit World
Dustland
The Gathering
The House of Dies Drear
In the Beginning: Creation Stories from Around the World
Junius Over Far
Justice and Her Brother
A Little Love
M.C. Higgins, the Great
The Magical Adventures of the Pretty Pearl
Many Thousand Gone: African Americans from Slavery to Freedom
The Mystery of Drear House
Plain City
Paul Robeson
The People Could Fly: American Black Tales
Planet of Junior Brown
Sheema, Queen of the Road
Sweet Whispers, Brother Rush
W.E.B. Dubois: A Biography
A White Romance
Willie Bea and the Time the Martians Landed
Zeely

Activities
Virginia Hamilton

1. Read about Tar Baby in *The People Could Fly: American Black Tales*. There are three hundred versions or variants of the Tar Baby story. Find a version from India, Brazil, Africa, or another country and compare.

2. Examine retellings of the Brer Rabbit tales done by Virginia Hamilton, Julius Lester, and others. Keep track of how many different names are used for Brer Rabbit. Riley is one. Try to find out why this famous literary trickster is called by different names.

3. Have students pretend they are conductors on the Underground Railroad directing slaves from the South to Yellow Springs, Ohio. Map the journey; discuss potential problems and solutions that both conductors and slaves might encounter. List some landmarks real or imagined along the way.

4. *Sweet Whispers, Brother Rush* has a ghost as a main character. His name is Brother Rush. Direct students who enjoyed this book to Richard Peck's novel, *The Ghost Belonged to Me*, where the main character is a girl ghost.

5. Remembering and knowing about our past is a message that Virginia Hamilton gives her readers. Have students talk about the country their ancestors came from and list people or events in family or national history which have made them feel proud of their heritage.

JAMAKE HIGHWATER

Jamake (pronounced juh-MAH-kuh) Highwater is a Native American of Blackfeet/Cherokee heritage. He was born on February 14, 1942 in Montana. His mother could neither read nor write but would tell Jamake stories about tribal life in the Indian world. Jamake's father was an Indian rodeo clown and rider who later became a stuntman for western movies. His work meant that the family traveled a great deal following the rodeo and movie location circuits. When Jamake was ten his father died in an automobile accident and because his mother was too poor to take care of him, he was adopted by his dad's best friend, an non-Indian whose last name was Marks. Jamake moved to California and became known as J. Marks, a name he used as a teenager and later as a pseudonym or pen name for several of his non-Indian books. He reverted to his real name in 1969 when he began work on his first 'Indian' book, a travel guide called *Indian America*.

Jamake did not always get along with his foster family in California, but there he did find three adults who influenced him in a positive way. The first were Mr. and Mrs Door, neighbors who allowed him to stay in their house whenever he wanted and introduced him to music, dance, and the world of books. The other adult was a social studies teacher named Alta Black who helped him with his school work and encouraged him to become a writer. It was she who gave him his first typewriter. Jamake did not like school and had no friends until Alta Black convinced him that she cared and approved of him. He went on to become an excellent student who found a way to go to college despite having very little money. Today he holds college degrees in music, literature, and anthropology.

At the beginning of his writing career Jamake wrote two books about rock music and Mick Jagger as well as many articles for various newspapers. Then in 1969, following the Indian invasion of Alcatraz Island in San Francisco Bay, his writing turned towards his own heritage. He produced books on Indian art, history, and in 1977 his first novel, *ANPAO: An American Indian Odyssey*, which was named a Newbery Honor Book in 1978. *Anpao* is the story of an Indian boy who must seek permission from the Sun to marry the girl he loves. The author weaves Indian legends into the adventures Anpao and his brother have as they travel to find the Sun.

Jamake Highwater went on to write several more novels for young people, a book of poetry (*Moonsong Lullaby*) and many books of non-fiction on Indian art and artists, history, dance, music, and ceremonies. Some of his books have been made into filmstrips that are available in schools and libraries. He also writes for television, popular magazines and newspapers, as well as books for adults.

Jamake has received many honors and awards for his writing and work on behalf of Native Americans. He has been named an honorary citizen of Oklahoma and in 1979 the Chief of the Blackfeet Indians honored him by giving him a new name, "Piitai Sahkomaapii," meaning "Eagle Son." This name-ceremony is usually reserved for children of the Blackfeet Nation but was given to Jamake to honor his achievements. Readers may now know this author by *three* names: Jamake Highwater, J. Marks, or Eagle Son.

A Selection of Books by Jamake Highwater

ANPAO: An American Indian Odyssey
The Ceremony of Innocence
Eyes of Darkness
I Wear the Morning Star
Kill Hole
Legend Days

Many Smokes, Many Moons:
A Chronology of American Indian History Through Indian Art

Moonsong Lullaby
Ritual of the Wind: Native American Painting
Song From the Earth: Native American Painting
The Sun He Dies: A Novel about the End of the Aztec World

Activities
Jamake Highwater

1. In his lovely poem *Moonsong Lullaby*, Jamake Highwater tells what the Moon celebrates during the night. Choose a nighttime song such as "Rock-a-Bye Baby" and write new words for it. Use words that the Moon might sing to the sun, to you, or to the rest of nature.

2. Use a scratchboard to create a peaceful "Moonsong Lullaby" picture. Use ideas from the book or other ideas of your own.

3. In Jamake Highwater's book *Legend Days*, the hero Amana must learn to keep her sacred gifts hidden. She must learn to cook, sew, help her sister and her elderly father. Write about her heroic qualities and how these qualities helped her.

4. In *Legend Days* Amana, Crow Woman, and Far Away Son speak of changes brought to their people by the White Men and their Great White Mother from England. Crow Woman sadly announces that, "I think it might be good that I vanish with the world I knew." Describe the changes she is talking about. Be sure to include changes in customs, nature, families, leaders, and religion.

5. Jamake Highwater's stories are filled with Native American names such as Jamie Ghost Horse, Henrietta White Calf, Far Away Son, Crow Woman, and Grandmother Yellow Bird Woman. Think about your friends and relatives; the way they look, the things they like, and what they like to do. Make up Native American names for them. Draw or paint pictures of them.

JULIUS LESTER

Master story teller, Julius Lester, has always loved books and reading. His library with its floor-to-ceiling bookshelves is located in the center of his house. He estimates that he owns between five and ten thousand books, most of which he has read. He thinks that he became a writer because he loves books and cannot imagine a life without them.

Julius Lester grew up in Kansas City, Kansas; Pine Bluff, Arkansas; and Nashville, Tennessee during a time when African American people were segregated from Caucasians. There were rules then on where

African Americans could eat, live, go to school, attend movies, or even use a library. Julius remembers being frightened by the restrictions and violence around him. Following high school he went to college, majoring in English because it allowed him to continue to read. He is currently a college professor at the University of Massachusetts in Amherst.

He writes at a typewriter in his home library while listening to rock music on the radio. The noise of his four children and the telephone do not bother him. Besides being a storyteller and college professor, he has also written songs, recorded albums and worked as a photographer. Artists like Tom Feelings and Jerry Pinkney who have their own chapters in the book you are now reading have illustrated his stories.

Julius Lester writes for children and adults and is most famous for retelling African folktales. He says that, "Folktales are a way to know any group of people." His Uncle Remus stories are authentic folktales originally told by slaves. Many of the Uncle Remus stories feature trickster Brer Rabbit as the main character.

In 1968 he published a book for young people on how it felt to be a slave. His research led him to the Library of Congress in Washington, D.C. where he read thousands of interviews from ex-slaves in order to better understand their language, speech patterns and feelings about slavery. *To Be a Slave*, a runner-up for the 1969 Newbery Medal was the result. This book is still in print and available in many libraries.

Julius Lester is of African and Jewish ancestry and he has also rewritten folktales from the Jewish tradition. Several can be found in his book, *How Many Spots Does a Leopard Have? & Other Tales*.

He feels that "Story is not something we tell. Story is something we are." His books proudly reflect who and what Julius Lester is.

A Selection of Books by
Julius Lester

Black Folktales

Further Tales of Uncle Remus:
The Misadventures of Brer Rabbit, Brer Fox, Brer Wolf, The Doodang
& All the Other Creatures

How Many Spots Does a Leopard Have? & Other Tales
The Knee-High Man & Other Tales

More Tales of Uncle Remus:
Further Adventures of Brer Rabbit, His Friends, Enemies & Others

The Tales of Uncle Remus: The Adventures of Brer Rabbit, Vol. 1
This Strange New Feeling
To Be a Slave
Who I Am

Activities
Julius Lester

1. Read the prologue in Lester's *To Be a Slave*, which is an actual account of slaves being seized and transported by ship to America. Compare it to the fictionalized account in Paula Fox's book, *The Slave Dancer*.

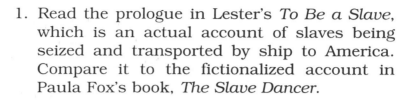

2. Make a story mural of several Brer Rabbit adventures. Display it in the hall or on a classroom bulletin board.

3. For creative writing or discussion, play the "What If" game. Ask students to think about what their lives would be like if they were slaves. "If I were a slave I would be living...wearing...working...etc."

4. Confront racism by examining stereotypes with humor. Examples: "Caucasians don't have rhythm," "separate but equal." Television is a good source for this assignment.

5. Write a character sketch of "Who I Am" in verse or narrative format inside the outline figure of yourself. Display on bulletin boards or hallways. May be life-size if space permits.

6. A newspaperman, Joel Chandler Harris, collected over two hundred Uncle Remus stories from black people over a hundred years ago. Many of the stories appeared in southern newspapers where they were very popular. Read one of the Uncle Remus stories and retell it in cartoon or comic strip format for the school or class newspaper.

PATRICIA McKISSACK

Patricia L'Ann Carwell was born in Nashville, Tennessee. Her mother and father both had civil servant jobs, which means they worked for the Government. One of the things Patricia remembers most about her childhood was listening to her grandfather tell stories to her and her sister, Sarah. He was a terrific storyteller and he made the stories come alive for the girls.

Patricia went to college and became a teacher. When she was twenty-one years old, she married Frederick McKissack. They have three sons who are grown-ups now: Frederick, and Robert and John, who are twins. Patricia and her husband work together on many book projects, though

Patricia also writes many books by herself. Their son Robert has helped with some of them. Today, they all live in St. Louis where Patricia teaches, and she and her husband own and operate a publishing company.

One of Patricia McKissack's most popular books is, *Flossie and the Fox*. She remembers her grandfather telling her this folktale when she was a little girl, but she loved it so much that she wanted to share it with her readers. Her grandfather's version of the story had a wolf, a bear, a snake, and a fox after poor Flossie, but Patricia changed it. She wanted the story to be simpler and she thought having just the sly fox trying to fool Flossie would be better. Her grandfather always told his stories using Patricia's and Sarah's names for the characters, but she changed that in her book, too. She thought "Flossie" and the Fox sounded much better than "Pat" and the Fox.

Patricia also remembers the special way her grandfather spoke. "Did I ever tell you 'bout the time..." he began. He had a smooth, musical way of talking that many people in the South have, and he made his stories special by putting southern words and expressions into them. Patricia tries to put her grandfather's "sound" into her books. She even uses some of his made-up words—like "disremember." (See if you can find others.)

Besides her own storybooks, Patricia and her husband together have written dozens of books on the lives of famous African American people who worked to make the United States a better place. It is important for people to have heroes they can look up to, and the women and men they have written about are surely heroes.

One of their books is about James Weldon Johnson, a famous African American man who was a lawyer, teacher, writer, musician, and government diplomat. One of the most famous songs Mr. Johnson wrote, and which his brother set to music, was selected by the National Association for the Advancement of Colored People (NAACP) to be its theme song. The song is called "Lift Every Voice and Sing."

Patricia McKissack wrote that Mr. Johnson's songs lifted people's spirits and filled their hearts with hope, courage, love, and joy. "There is no greater way to be remembered." The same thing could be said about Patricia McKissack: Her books lift people's spirits and fill them with hope, courage, love, and joy.

A Selection of Books Written by
Patricia McKissack

The Apache
Aztec Indians
Bugs! Insectos!
Carter G. Woodson: The Father of Black History
The Dark Thirty: Southern Tales of the Supernatural
Flossie and the Fox
Frederick Douglass: Leader Against Slavery
George Washington Carver: The Peanut Scientist
Give It With Love, Christopher
Ida B. Wells-Barnett: A Voice Against Violence
James Weldon Johnson: Lift Every Voice and Sing
Jesse Jackson: A Biography
The King's New Clothes
The Little Red Hen
Los Incas
Los Mayas
Marian Anderson: A Great Singer
Martin Luther King, Jr: A Man to Remember
Messy Bessey's Garden
Michael Jackson: Superstar
Monkey-Monkey's Trick
Nettie Jo's Friends
Sojourner Truth: Ain't I A Woman?
Who Is Who?

Activities
Patricia McKissack

1. Patricia McKissack chose the name "Flossie" for her story of *Flossie and the Fox* because she liked the way the two names sounded together.

   Try to match other names that sound good together and then write a story about them. Here are some to get you started:

   > Gertrude and the Goat
   > Donna and the Duck
   > Henry and the Horse
   > Paddy and the Penguin

2. In the book *Long Hard Journey: The Story of the Pullman Porter*, Patricia and her husband told about railroad workers long ago. Read books from your library that tell about the early days of other industries: airlines, ocean liners, bus companies, and space travel. How were the equipment and work different from today? Create time-lines showing important dates in those businesses.

3. Read several of the biographies written by Patricia McKissack and her husband. Make a list of the personal characteristics those people had. Do some of the characteristics appear on more than one list? Why? Write a composition about what you think a person must be like in order to help improve the lives of other people.

4. Patricia McKissack uses lots of made-up words that she heard her grandfather use in stories. See how many words like "disremember" that you can make up. Words such as disinvited, reunliking, unbelonged...

WALTER DEAN MYERS

Walter Dean Myers was born in the small town of Martinsburg, West Virginia in 1937. There were many children in his family and when his mother died, his father had trouble caring for the children by himself. The Dean family, who were friends of Walter's dead mother, offered to adopt him and the father agreed. The Deans lived in Harlem, New York and that is where Walter spent most of his childhood.

Adjusting to a big city and his foster parents was not difficult because he loved his new life, although as a very young child Walter had a severe speech problem and would sometimes fight and misbehave in school when other children teased him about the way he spoke. Harlem, during Walter's childhood was not an urban crime-filled ghetto, but a place where young people played basketball and stickball outdoors, went to church, sat on fire escapes to find relief from warm apartments, and listened to stories at the public library. Famous African American poet, Langston Hughes, lived only a few blocks away and world champion fighter, Sugar Ray Robinson, shadow boxed with Walter and his friends on the streets. This life is what he tries to portray in his books when he writes about the African American experience as he knew it.

Walter Dean Myers is a versatile writer and not all his books are set in Harlem or are about African Americans. He received many awards for his Vietnam War novel, *Fallen Angels*, and for younger readers he has written two novels about kids and Little League baseball, *Me, Mop and the Moondance Kid* and *Mop, Moondance, and the Nagasaki Knights*.

Walter Dean Myers has three children and lives in Jersey City, New Jersey just across the river from New York City. He works at home and makes his living as a full-time writer of books for young and teenage readers. He says that he "loves being a writer and thinks that it is God's gift to him. I write to give hope to those kids who are like the one I knew—poor, troubled, treated indifferently by society, sometimes bolstered by family and many times not."

A Selection of Books by
Walter Dean Myers

Ambush in the Amazon
The Black Pearl and the Ghost
Brown Angels: An Album of Pictures and Verse
Crystal
The Dragon Takes a Wife
Fallen Angels
Fast Sam, Cool Clyde & Stuff
The Golden Serpent
The Hidden Shrine
Hoops
It Ain't all for Nothin'
The Legend of Tarik
Malcolm X: By Any Means Necessary
Me, Mop & the Moondance Kid
Mop, Moondance, and the Nagasaki Knights
Motown and Didi: A Love Story
The Mouse Rap
Mr. Monkey and the Gotcha Bird
The Nicholas Factor
The Outside Shot
Scorpions
Sweet Illusions
Won't Know Till I Get There
The Young Landlords
Somewhere in the Darkness
Young Martin's Promise

Activities
Walter Dean Myers

1. *The Dragon Takes A Wife* by Myers is a modern African American fairy tale. Read this amusing tale aloud and ask students to modernize another familiar fairy or folk tale. Try adding rap language/lyrics to the story.

2. Looking for a different way of book reporting? Read a Myers teen-age novel and ask the reader to compare it to his/her teen-age experiences.

3. Inner-city life is often dramatized by this author. Clip photos from newspapers and magazines to create a collage that reflects a realistic look at urban life and activities today.

4. *The Legend of Tarik*, by Meyers and *The High King*, by Lloyd Alexander have heroes with much in common. Serious readers, sixth grade and up might enjoy reading both and comparing Taran and Tarik.

5. Myers writes about teen-age gangs in *Scorpions*, a Newbery Honor book, through the words of the Scorpions themselves. This same technique and message was used in another older book, *The Outsiders*, by S.E. Hinton. It can be highly recommended.

6. *Brown Angels: An Album of Pictures and Verse*, is a collection of old photographs of African American children accompanied by original poems. Collect old photographs and make a classroom album project of the pictures. Ask each student to select a photograph and write a poem or story about the person in the picture. Save the album for creative writing and social studies discussions.

BRIAN PINKNEY

Once when Brian Pinkney was a boy, he went to an African dance performance. When he got home he painted a picture of a dancer leaping through the air. His parents liked the painting so much that they had it framed and hung it up in their home. This was a very big compliment for Brian because his mother was a writer and his father was a famous children's book illustrator. They knew their son had talent.

While he was growing up, Brian enjoyed making model planes and cars. He often went to the library to read books about building things. Most important, he enjoyed painting pictures. He was able to teach himself a great deal about painting, but his father gave him helpful suggestions as he went along. In grammar school his teachers had him make posters for extra credit. They knew he had talent, too.

Brian grew up in Massachusetts and was one of only a few African American children in his school. Now, he says, he likes to illustrate and write books about being African American. Brian studied painting at the Fine Arts University in Philadelphia and did his graduate studies at the School of Visual Arts in New York City.

You will love Brian Pinkney's illustrations. For his first book, *The Boy and the Ghost*, he used swirly watercolor paints. After that book he began experimenting with other techniques, especially black-and-white scratchboard prints. He sometimes adds oil paint to these prints to give them more feeling.

Today, Brian works closely with his wife, Andrea, who has written some of the stories he has illustrated. They talk over the plans for a book for a long time before he starts doing the rough sketches. When he shows these to Andrea, they talk about them some more. Then he spends many hours preparing the finished artwork. Andrea is the one who helps him the most with his art.

Brian Pinkney is very happy with his life. He works in his studio at home every day except Saturday. He works mostly at night so he can have fun during the day. When he gets stuck for ideas he goes to a movie, plays the drums, reads a book, or takes a nap. "I get a lot of good ideas after a twenty minute nap."

Brian especially enjoys illustrating stories about African American characters. When he studies for a book project he feels that he learns, not only about the story characters and the places where they live, but also about himself. What he learns about himself he puts back into his art. "I make pictures for the child in me."

That must be why children of all ages—from eight years old to eighty—enjoy Brian Pinkney's work so much!

A Selection of Books Illustrated by
Brian Pinkney

The Ballad of Belle Dorcas
The Boy and the Ghost
The Dark Thirty: Southern Tales of the Supernatural
The Dream Keeper and Other Poems
The Elephant's Wrestling Match
Harriet Tubman and Black History Month
Julie Brown: Racing Against the Wind
The Lost Zoo
Seven Candles for Kwanzaa
A Wave in Her Pocket
Where Does the Trail Lead?

Activities
Brian Pinkney

1. Brian Pinkney used a scratchboard technique for the illustrations in *Where Does the Trail Lead?* You can make scratchboard pictures without any special equipment. You only need some paper, some crayons, and lots of imagination.

   Think of a picture you would like to draw. Now take a piece of white construction paper and, with your crayons, color all over it with patches of bright colors. Lean on the crayons pretty hard so none of the paper shows through. Next, color over those colors with a black crayon so that none of the colors show through. Now you are ready to make your "scratchboard" picture appear.

   Use a toothpick, the tip of your scissors, or some other object to make your picture appear by scratching off the black crayon. Be careful not to scratch off the colored crayon underneath. The patches of colors that you put on the paper first will add interesting surprises to your drawing.

2. Brian Pinkney illustrated Robert D. San Souci's book, *The Boy and the Ghost.* By his courage and kindness, Thomas helps put the Ghost's body back together again. You can have fun putting pieces back together, too.

   Draw a scene from the story on a piece of large drawing paper. Ask your teacher to laminate your drawing. (This helps keep the pieces neat. You can still do the project if it can't be laminated.) Next, cut the drawing

into six or eight pieces to make your own jigsaw puzzle. As you get better at doing the puzzle you can cut it into more pieces, but it's best to start out with just a few.

You can make additional puzzles out of other drawings or photographs.

3. Divide four sheets of paper into thirds like the example. On each sheet draw a creature so that the head, the body, and the legs are in each section of the paper. Staple the sheets together and cut them into thirds, but do NOT cut them all the way through. Now you can flip the papers to match different heads with different bodies and legs. (If you have a computer, you can also do this with the "Creature Maker" game on the *Print Shop Companion* disk.)

4. In *The Boy and the Ghost*, Thomas was rewarded for helping the ghost. He dug up the earthen pot filled with gold and silver coins. He shared half of it with the poor and brought the rest home to his family.

Everyone has their own idea for what would be their best hidden treasure. For one person it might be money. For another it might be...What?

Write a story about how you discover a hidden treasure. When you open the treasure chest, what do you find? What do you do with it? How does the treasure change your life? Illustrate your story.

JERRY PINKNEY

Jerry Pinkney was born in Philadelphia, Pennsylvania in 1939. Jerry's father was a talented man who did lots of different kinds of jobs. He was a painter, a plumber, a gardener, and an electrician. His mother and father encouraged Jerry to do whatever he was good at. What he was good at was art.

When Jerry was growing up, his two older brothers enjoyed drawing and Jerry thinks some of this rubbed off on him. He was not a very good reader in school, but he soon discovered that he was good at drawing. His teachers noticed this and they often let him complete his assignments using artwork in some way. Before he knew it, he became known as the "class artist."

When Jerry was eleven years old, he had a newspaper stand on a busy street corner. He kept his sketchpad with him, so he could draw when there weren't any customers. A famous cartoonist saw his drawings and invited Jerry to visit his nearby studio. The artist gave him lots of pencils, paper, and erasers. From seeing this man's studio, Jerry understood that people can earn a living with their art. He knew that he wanted to be an artist when he grew up.

Jerry took several art classes and learned all he could about drawing, painting, lettering, and designing. Usually he was the only African American student in the classes and he realized that all people are different and have different talents.

When he graduated from high school, Jerry won a scholarship to attend the Philadelphia Museum College of Art. After college, Jerry married a woman named Gloria whom he had known since high school. By the time he was twenty-three years old, he and Gloria had four children who have also turned out to be talented people. (You can read about their son Brian Pinkney in this book, too.)

When he graduated from college, Jerry worked in a flower shop while he began his art career. Next he got a job as an artist at a greeting card company in Boston. During his vacations, Jerry traveled to New York City showing his artwork to editors at magazine and book publishing companies. His first book project was to illustrate a book called *The Adventures of Spider.*

When he starts a book project, Jerry does a lot of research at museums and libraries to learn as much as he can about the people and places in the book. He starts with some rough sketches before he goes on to the finished watercolor paintings. He often uses live models to pose certain scenes from the story so he can see what their gestures would be like. His wife, Gloria, has posed for him many times. So have his children and other family members. Besides using watercolor paints, Jerry also uses ink, colored pencils, Cray-Pas, and pastels.

Jerry's studio is right in his home. He teaches college students a couple of days a week, but on the other days he works on his book projects.

Creating artwork is very hard work, but since it gives Jerry so much pleasure, it is more like play. Jerry Pinkney uses his mind, his heart, and his talents to create beautiful pictures that are loved by millions of people all over the world.

A Selection of Books Illustrated or Written by Jerry Pinkney

Back Home
Great Minu
The Green Lion of Zion Street
Half a Moon and One Whole Star
Home Place
I Want to Be
J.D.
Kasho and the Twin Flutes
Kostas the Rooster
The Man Who Kept His Heart in a Bucket
Mildred Murphy, How Does Your Garden Grow?
Mirandy and Brother Wind
The Patchwork Quilt
The Planet of Junior Brown
Pretend You're a Cat
Rabbit Makes a Monkey of Lion: A Swahili Tale
Song of the Trees
A Starlit Somersault Downhill
Tales of Uncle Remus: The Adventures of Brer Rabbit
Talking Eggs: A Folktale from the American South
Tonweya and the Eagles, and Other Lakota Indian Tales
Traveling Frog
Turtle in July
Yagua Days
Wild, Wild Sunflower Child Anna

Activities
Jerry Pinkney

1. Jerry Pinkney illustrated Mildred D. Taylor's book, *Song of the Trees*. Go outside and look at the trees. Pick one tree and sit under it. Draw a picture of what the tree looks like looking up into it from where you are sitting. If you can climb the tree, go up into its branches and draw what you see looking out from where you are sitting. Write a poem about your "Tree Friend."

2. Jerry Pinkney's illustrations in *The Talking Eggs,* show the beautiful colors of the different-colored chickens and the odd two-headed cow with the corkscrew horns. Try to imagine a new animal and draw a picture of it. Draw a duck with the nose and tail of a pig. Draw a feathered horse with the horns of a cow. Draw a fish with the long legs and tail of a horse. Invent your own animals and draw a picture of them. Then write a story about them.

3. Jerry Pinkney has designed stamps for the United States Postal Service. Your mom and dad are the real stars in your life. Design a stamp for them and draw it on a large piece of paper. Be sure to put the scalloped edges on it, just like on real stamps. Write a composition about your parents telling why they should be on a stamp.

4. Make up math problems about stamps you collect from the mail. Glue several stamps onto a piece of construction paper. Other students have to compute the value of all the stamps on the paper.

5. Write other math stamp problems like this one:

   If Jerry bought three 29-cent stamps, and five 16-cent stamps, how much change would he get if he paid with a five-dollar bill?

6. Jerry Pinkney illustrated Valerie Flourney's book, *The Patchwork Quilt*. In the story, Grandma tells Tanya it would take her a year to make a quilt for her, but that it would be a masterpiece.

   Make enough construction paper squares (6" x 6") for each member of your class to design enough squares to make a "quilt." Glue the squares onto a piece of a roll of construction paper. Hang the quilt in the hall for everyone to see. People will say it's "nothin' but a joy!"

7. Cartoonists tell stories with words and simple pictures. Fold a piece of paper so you have eight boxes. Retell the story of *The Talking Eggs*, with cartoon drawings.

ALLEN SAY

Allen Say was born in Yokohama, Japan. He came to live in the United States when he was sixteen years old. He was an artist when he arrived and, even though it has not always been easy, he has remained an artist ever since.

His mother and father discouraged Allen from becoming an artist. They believed that all artists were poor and dirty. They told Allen that if he became an artist he would never have a job, a home, or a family of his own. They told him he would never be happy. Allen was determined to become an artist and to prove to his parents that artists can be just as happy as doctors, lawyers, teachers, carpenters, scientists, or anybody else.

When Allen came to California, he also faced other difficulties. Not only was he an unknown young man trying to become an artist against his parents' wishes, but everybody he met saw him as an outsider who did not belong. Here was a young man coming from a far-off country who had a Japanese mother and a Korean father—how would he ever be able to blend in with everybody else? With all his might, Allen tried to blend in.

Allen Say began writing and illustrating children's books when he was thirty-five years old. His first book was called *Dr. Smith's Safari.* None of the characters were Oriental people. Even the main character's name was very American: Dr. Smith.

Soon Allen began to use stories from his childhood for his books. He thought this might help explain his background to other people and help them to understand him a little better and not think of him as an "outsider" anymore.

He told the story of *The Bicycle Man,* which takes place right after World War II when there were still American soldiers in Japan. The hero is an American black man. Even though the people cannot speak to each other because they do not know each other's language, they are still able to communicate. They share the gift of friendship anyway.

Being accepted by others became such a problem for Allen that he decided to give up working on children's books altogether. He did not think it was possible to convince other people that he was not just an "Oriental" but that he was a regular person just like everyone else.

Before he gave up, Allen was talked into working on just one more book, *The Boy of the Three-Year Nap,* written by Diane Snyder. A kind of miracle happened. He loved the project so much that he decided to create children's books for the rest of his life! From then on, his books have shown characters who are comfortable being who they are, wherever they are, just the way they are.

Millions of Allen Say's readers are happy that he still creates books. It does not matter whether their skin is black, brown, red, white, or yellow. They simply love his books.

In January 1994, Allen Say won the prestigious Caldecott Medal for his book, *Grandfather's Journey.* We are glad that Allen Say decided to pursue his work creating children's books.

A Selection of Books Written or Illustrated by
Allen Say

The Bicycle Man
The Boy of the Three-Year Nap
Dr. Smith's Safari
El Chino
The Feast of Lanterns
Grandfather's Journey
How My Parents Learned to Eat
The Innkeeper's Apprentice
The Lost Lake
Magic and the Night River
Once Under the Cherry Blossom Tree
A River Dream
Tree of Cranes

Activities
Allen Say

1. After you have read, *A River Dream*, pretend that the street in front of your house has turned into a river and your bicycle has become a rowboat. Where would you go? What adventures would you have? Write your own story and draw you own pictures for your very own "River Dream."

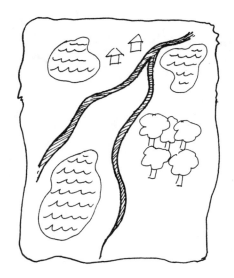

2. After you read, *Lost Lake*, look at a map and find the names of lakes and rivers in your area. Write the names of five of them. Ask a friend to put them in alphabetical order.

3. After reading, *Lost Lake*, photocopy or draw a map with the lakes or rivers in your area. Play a map game with a partner. Put a penny on the map. Now choose a lake, but do not tell your partner the name of it. Give directions to the lake that will help your partner name it: "It's north of the penny. It's south of the railroad." Take turns.

4. After reading, *The Bicycle Man*, hold a "Parade of Bicycles" at your next school or town celebration. Use streamers, flowers, and balloons to decorate your bikes. Instead, you might draw pictures of fancy bikes and decorate them with tiny colorful tissue paper flowers.

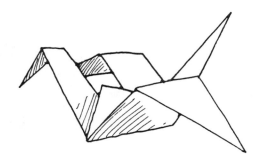

5. After reading, *Tree of Cranes*, borrow several origami books from your library. Learn how to make a dove or a paper crane. (The crane is a bit difficult for a beginner.) Origami will teach you patience, concentration, and accuracy. You will also have a feeling of peaceful accomplishment.

MILDRED D. TAYLOR

Mildred D. Taylor was born in Jackson, Mississippi at a time when African American people in America were still struggling for full freedom. When she was three months old, her parents moved with Mildred and her sister to Ohio.

When she was going to school in the 1940's and 1950's, Mildred disliked the way African American history was taught. She believed that it did not tell the way things really were. What she heard in school did not sound anything like the history she learned from her father and her grandfather.

Mildred's father was a master storyteller. The Taylor family often sat spellbound in front of the fireplace or on the front porch under the moonlight listening to the stories of African American people who lived their lives with pride and dignity. These were stories of real people who had lived in Ohio and Mississippi. Some of the stories had been passed down through generations, from the time of slavery. Mildred became inspired by the heroes of these stories. Their example taught her to love and respect herself, her family, and her heritage.

After college, Mildred worked in Ethiopia for two years with the Peace Corps. Her stay there taught her more about what life was like for African American people before they were brought to America as slaves. When she returned to the United States, she received a Masters degree from the University of Colorado.

Her father's stories had become such a part of her that Mildred wanted to put them down on paper. Her first attempt was a story called "The Friendship" which she did not publish for many years. She did not feel that on paper it had the power it had when she heard it told by her father. She decided not to publish it until it was strong enough to give the reader the same kind of response she felt when she first heard the story as a little girl. She wanted to be sure that the reader would feel sadness and outrage at the unjust treatment the character Mr. Tom Bee had received just because of the color of his skin, and to feel admiration for his courage and dignity in the face of discrimination. When *The Friendship* was ready to do all that, it was published and won several important awards.

Mildred Taylor won the coveted Newbery Award in 1977 for *Roll of Thunder, Hear My Cry*. In this story told by the character Cassie Logan, Mildred used memories from her own childhood, especially the love and devotion her family shared.

Mildred Taylor loves her work. She is also very happy to share it with millions of other people. She hopes that her books will provide children today with the kind of heroes that were missing from books when she was a girl.

Mildred D. Taylor's deceased father would be very proud of his daughter. Like him, she has become a Master Storyteller.

A Selection of Books Written by
Mildred D. Taylor

The Friendship
The Gold Cadillac
Let the Circle Be Unbroken
Mississippi Bridge
The Road to Memphis
Roll of Thunder, Hear My Cry
Song of the Trees

Activities:
Mildred D. Taylor

1. Ask one of your parents or grandparents to tell you a story from their childhood. Listen very carefully and then write it down in your own words. Illustrate your story. Make a class book of your family stories and tape record them. Invite the story tellers to visit your class to listen to their stories as you tell them.

2. Research the life of a famous African American or someone who worked for the rights of African Americans. Make a class book of these life stories. Make a bulletin board display to honor these heroic women and men.

3. After reading some of Mildred D. Taylor's books, make a list of ways the characters were treated unjustly. Next to each one, write how things are different today. Make another list of ways that people today still treat others unjustly. Next to each one, write how things should be.

4. Read the "I Have a Dream" speech by Martin Luther King, Jr. Write a story about your dream for humanity. Make a bulletin board display with drawings and paintings of your dreams.

5. Mildred was born in Mississippi. Make up a list of names and state names that start with the same letter. Names such as Wesley Wyoming, Mary Montana, etc.

6. Write a story of your own titled "The Friendship." It can be real or imaginary.

YOSHIKO UCHIDA

Yoshiko Uchida grew up in Berkeley, California where she lived with her parents and sister, Keiko, in a home that was frequently filled with visitors from Japan. Her parents had been born in Japan and had left behind many friends who would visit the Uchidas when they came to America.

Yoshiko (later shortened to Yoshi) was born in the United States, attended schools here and felt very American. She visited Japan twice when she was a child but felt like a foreigner there.

Yet, a large part of her was Japanese because her parents had passed on to her so much of their culture. She realized that when she returned to Japan as an adult in 1952. She knew then, that as a child she had pushed away her ethnicity in her eagerness to be accepted as an American, but that everything she admired and loved about Japan was a part of her and always had been. Later she was to write about the "invisible thread" of Japan in her autobiography.

Yoshiko always wanted to be a teacher. Young Yoshi would sit at her desk, take attendance of her imaginary class and pretend to teach her pupils how to spell, write, and read. She began to write short stories in the sixth grade but didn't consider writing as a career until she was an adult. Because there were very few teaching jobs for Japanese Americans, Yoshiko didn't study education when she entered the university.

Just five months before her college graduation, the Uchida's lives changed drastically. In December, 1941 Japan bombed Pearl Harbor, Hawaii in a surprise attack. Afterwards, Japanese Americans were treated as dangerous non-aliens and many, including the Uchida's were evacuated to prisoner-of-war camps in other states. There they lived behind barbed wire fences and locked gates, guarded by armed soldiers.

In the camps, Yoshiko taught school, learned how to knit, read every book she could find, wrote letters, and was very homesick for California.

She and her sister wrote many letters asking for permission to attend a college outside the camp. Eventually their clearance letters arrived and they were allowed to leave. The two sisters traveled by train from Utah and the internment camp to Massachusetts and a college campus.

In 1944 Yoshiko received her master's degree in education and began teaching the first and second grades at a Quaker school outside Philadelphia. Both grades met in the same classroom. She remembers twenty-four smiling students rushing into the room that first day, scrambling for seats, and herself saying, "Good morning, boys and girls. My name is Miss Uchida, and I am going to be your teacher." Her dream to become a real teacher had finally come true.

Yoshiko Uchida has published three collections of Japanese folk tales and written several books about Japanese children for young readers. Not surprisingly, many of her stories have school settings. She also has written three books about her experiences in the internment camps during World War II.

She says in her autobiography, *The Invisible Thread*, that she "hopes young people who read her books will dare to have big dreams." She wants them to love and cherish their freedom and their own special heritage whatever it is.

A Selection of Books by Yoshiko Uchida

The Best Bad Thing
The Birthday Visitor
The Bracelet
The Dancing Kettle
The Happiest Ending
The Invisible Thread: A Memoir by Yoshiko Uchida
A Jar of Dreams
Journey Home
Journey to Topaz
The Magic Listening Cap
The Magic Purse
Makoto, the Smallest Boy
The Promised Year
The Rooster Who Understood Japanese
Sumi and the Goat and the Tokyo Express
Sumi's Prize
Sumi's Special Happening
Sumurai of Gold Hill
Tabi: Journey Through Time
The Two Foolish Cats

Activities
Yoshiko Uchida

1. Yoshiko Uchida's family lived through a tragic period of American history. They and thousands of other Japanese Americans were victims of stereotypical prejudice, loss of jobs, forced relocations and internment in United States concentration camps. Research the rights and privileges of native and naturalized United States citizens. Debate whether the rights of Japanese Americans were violated in the 1940's.

2. Related research topics for further study on this subject are:
   The War Relocation Authority
   U.S. Concentration Camps in Topaz, Utah and other sites
   The All-Nisei 442nd Regimental Combat Team
   The 100th U.S. Army Infantry Battalion
   The 1988 Redress Bill

3. "The Tongue-Cut Sparrow," a Japanese folk tale retold by Yoshiko Uchida in, *The Dancing Kettle,* is a story of human greed and kindness rewarded. It can be easily adapted in dramatization by a small group or "Reader's Theater." An old man and woman, a small bird, and a treasure chest are the story components. Kimonos and obis (sash/belts) would make wonderful costumes.

4. After reading and listening to several Japanese stories, help students make simple origami figures of story parts; birds, fish, butterflies, kites, mice, flowers, and monkeys are suggestions. Invite an origami hobbyist from the community to assist. Origami figures make lovely holiday decorations. Easy origami instructions can be found in *Beautiful Origami,* by Zulal Ayture-Scheele, (Sterling, 1990) and *Easy Origami* by Dokuohtei Nakano, (Viking Kestrel, 1985).

5. *The Magic Purse* is the retelling of an old Japanese tale of kindness rewarded by the gift of a constantly refilling magic purse. As a class project practice random acts of kindness for a set period of time—at least a week. Keep a record and place foil-wrapped gold coin chocolate candy into a container for each recorded act. At the end of the project let your class enjoy their "kindness rewarded."

6. The Japanese *Magic Purse* story has much in common with the magic cooking pot stories from other countries and cultures. Read some of these and decide which would be better to have: a magic cooking pot or magic purse and why?

ED YOUNG

Ed Young was born in Tientsin, China during a time when there were great troubles there. He grew up at the edge of the city of Shanghai surrounded by farms, animals, and people. His father, Q.L. Young, was a professor of engineering at St. John's University in Shanghai. His mother, Tang Yuen, was an artist.

Ed was one of five children. His family's home, located on Tung Sing Road between the British Embassy and the Italian Embassy, was always a busy but happy place. All different types of people—young and old, Chinese or not—were welcome there. Since the house could be quite noisy, Ed often went off to a quiet room to entertain himself with good books and imaginary games.

Ed and his friends used to play drawing games together. His parents knew that Ed had talent and they encouraged him with his art. He often drew pictures of whatever came into his mind: people, airplanes, ships, and animals.

When Ed was twenty years old, he came to the United States on a scholarship to study architecture at the University of Illinois. After a couple of years, he decided to study art at the Art Center School in Los Angeles. When he graduated, he moved to New York City where he hoped to have a career as an artist.

Ed Young is fond of re-telling old, familiar stories while adding fresh, unique illustrations. Since Ed is an oriental person living in the United States, he has been able to mix the best of two different cultures into his art. As a result, his work has received many awards. *Lon Po Po*, Ed's retelling of a Red-Riding Hood story from China was awarded the Caldecott Medal in 1990. The book's unusual dedication to the wolf shows the artist's great respect for all creatures.

Ed Young does not have any real favorites of the many books he has illustrated. He told us that the one he is working on at the moment is his favorite because he is "still growing with it." As he affects the artwork, the artwork affects him. His artwork helps him to grow as a person.

When he was still a little boy in China, Ed Young used to wish that he could make magic like Walt Disney. In at least one way his wish has come true. Over the last thirty years, his beautiful artwork has magically enchanted readers of all ages and will continue to do so for many more years to come.

A Selection of Books Written or Illustrated by
Ed Young

All of You Was Singing
Bicycle Rider
Birches
The Bird From the Sea
Cats Are Cats
Chinese Mother Goose Rhymes
The Double Life of Pocahontas
The Emperor and the Kite
Eyes of the Dragon
The First Song Ever Sung
Foolish Rabbits' Big Mistake
The Happy Prince
High in the Mountains
The Horse From Nowhere
I Wish I Were a Butterfly
In the Night, Still Dark
The Girl Who Loved the Wind
Lon Po Po, A Red-Riding Hood Story from China
The Mean Mouse and Other Mean Stories
Mice Are Nice
Moon Mother
The Other Bone
Poetry for Young Scientists
Red Thread
Seven Blind Mice
The Seventh Mandarin
The Tiniest Sound
Up a Tree
While I Sleep
Who-Paddled-Backward-With-Trout
The Yellow Boat
Young Fu of the Upper Yangtze

Activities
Ed Young

1. Ed Young's artwork for Mary Calhoun's book, *While I Sleep,* is "lullaby-lovely."

   Read other books and find out how elephants, ducks, monkeys, crocodiles, hippos, and other animals sleep. Draw a picture and write a sentence for each.

   Where would your bicycle sleep? Your dolls? Your rollerskates? Where would a car sleep? A skateboard? A surfboard? Draw a picture and write a sentence for each.

   Now put your pictures and sentences together to make your own *While I Sleep* book. Design a dreamy cover that will wake everyone up to read your book.

2. Read *The Emperor and the Kite.* Draw a large diamond shape on a piece of paper and decorate it to look like a fancy kite. You can use construction paper and hang it on the wall or you can use brightly-colored tissue paper and hang it on a window to catch the sunlight passing through it.

3. Read Ed Young's *Seven Blind Mice.* Choose another animal story such as "The Three Little Pigs" and change the animals and the setting to make a whole new story, such as "The Five Big Pigs" or "Goldilocks and the Six Foxes." Create a cartoon comic strip for your story by dividing a piece of paper into twelve boxes and drawing pictures to illustrate it.

4. *Lon Po Po,* is a Red-Riding Hood story which came from China. Look in an atlas to find China on a map. Use the map and look in books to find the following information:

   How many miles away is China from the United States? In what hemisphere is China? What is the population of China? Write the names of five cities in China. What countries are China's neighbors? Write questions of your own about China for a friend to answer.

5. Read, *I Wish I Were a Butterfly.* Write a story of your own with the same title. Make a class book of different *If I Were...* stories.